Easy Greek Recipes You'll Love

The Best Authentic Greek Cookbook from the Mediterranean

BY: Alicia T. White

License Note!

Table of Contents

Introduction

If there is a culinary style that is both refined and bursting with flavorful ingredients, it is Greek food. Greek cooking is not something that can be taught by reading a couple of cookbooks, but it can be taught if you have the appropriate instructor. This style of food is really simple to create and will wow your friends and family with your cooking talents as long as you are eager to learn and have the right cooking gear.

If you've ever desired to master the art of Greek cooking, *"Easy Greek Recipes You'll Love"* is the cookbook for you. Inside this all-inclusive Greek cookbook, you'll find simple Greek recipes that will transform your cooking. You may become a Greek chef in a couple of days if you have access to more than 25 recipes.

Let's quit playing around and get to work on dinner!

OOOOOOOOOOOOOOOOOOOOOOOOOOOOOOOOOOOOOOOOOOOOO

1. Greek Cream Cheese Lemon Coffee Cake

Yield: 16 servings

Cooking Time: 55 minutes

Ingredients for the Cheese Layer:

- 8 ounces of Greek yogurt cream cheese, soft
- ¼ cup of white sugar
- 1 egg, beaten
- 1 ½ teaspoon of lemon juice

Ingredients for the Cake:

- 1 ½ cups of all-purpose flour
- ½ cup of vegetable oil
- ½ teaspoons baking powder
- ¾ cup of white sugar
- ¼ teaspoons baking soda
- 1 egg, beaten
- ¼ teaspoons of salt
- ½ cup of Greek yogurt
- 1 lemon, zest only
- 1 tablespoon of lemon juice

Ingredients for the Topping:

- ½ cup of all-purpose flour
- ¼ cup of white sugar
- 2 tablespoons of butter, cold and cut into small cubes
- Powdered sugar, for dusting

ooooooooooooooooooooooooooooooooooooooooooooooo

Procedure:

A. Preheat the oven to 350°F. Line a large baking dish with a sheet of parchment paper. Grease with cooking spray.

B. In a medium bowl, add the softened cream cheese, white sugar, beaten egg, and fresh lemon juice. Beat with an electric mixer until creamy in consistency. Set this mixture aside.

C. In a separate medium bowl, add the all-purpose flour, salt, baking powder, and soda. Stir well to mix and set this mixture aside.

D. In the large bowl of a stand mixer, add the vegetable oil, white sugar, and beaten egg. Beat on the lowest setting until mixed. Add in the yogurt, fresh lemon zest, and fresh lemon juice. Continue to beat until creamy in consistency.

E. Add in the flour mixture and continue to beat until just mixed.

F. Pour the batter into the prepared baking dish. Spread the cream cheese mixture over the top.

G. In a medium bowl, add ½ cup of all-purpose flour, ¼ cup of white sugar, and cold butter. Cut with a pastry cutter until crumbly in consistency. Spread over the top of the batter.

H. Place into the oven to bake for 40 to 45 minutes. Remove and dust immediately with powdered sugar. Serve.

2. Greek Gyro Skillet

Yield: 4 servings

Cooking Time: 50 minutes

Ingredient List:

- 2 chicken breasts, chopped into small pieces
- 3 tablespoons of extra virgin olive oil, evenly divided
- A dash of salt and black pepper
- 3 cloves of garlic, minced and evenly divided
- 1 teaspoon of dried oregano
- ½ of red onion, chopped
- 2 zucchinis, sliced into rounds
- 1 red bell pepper, sliced
- ½ teaspoons of dried dill
- ½ teaspoons of smoked paprika
- 1 ½ cups of long-grain white rice
- 3 cups of chicken broth
- ½ of a lemon, juice only
- ½ cup of grape tomatoes, cut into halves
- 1 cucumber, chopped
- ¼ cup of Kalamata olives, cut into halves
- 1/3 cup of feta cheese, crumbled
- 1 tablespoon of dill, chopped
- Lemon wedges, for serving

OOOOOOOOOOOOOOOOOOOOOOOOOOOOOOOOOOOOOOOOOO

Procedure:

In a medium bowl, add the chicken breasts, minced garlic, and a teaspoon of dried oregano. Season with a dash of salt and black pepper.

In a large skillet set over medium heat, add the olive oil. Once hot, add in the chicken breasts. Cook for 8 to 10 minutes or until golden brown. Remove and set aside on a plate to rest for 10 minutes.

Add another tablespoon of olive oil. Once hot, add in the onions and red bell pepper slices. Stir well to mix. Cook for 5 minutes or until soft.

Add in the zucchini rounds and continue to cook for another 5 minutes or until soft.

Add another tablespoon of the oil to the skillet. Once hot, add in the remaining clove of garlic, dried fill, and smoked paprika. Cook for 1 minute or until fragrant. Add in the white rice, chicken broth, and fresh lemon juice. Bring this mixture to a boil.

Cover and reduce the heat to low. Cook for 15 to 20 minutes or until the rice is cooked through.

Add in the chopped grape tomatoes, chopped cucumber, Kalamata olive halves, crumbled feta cheese, and dill. Stir well to mix.

Serve with chicken and lemon wedges.

3. Greek Stuffed Bell Peppers

Yield: 6 servings

Cooking Time: 1 hour and 20 minutes

Ingredient List:

- 6 red bell peppers
- 1 tablespoon of extra virgin olive oil
- 1 pound of chicken breasts, boneless and skinless
- 1 teaspoon of dried oregano
- A dash of salt and black pepper
- 1 ½ cup of low sodium chicken broth
- 1 cup of couscous
- 1 red onion, chopped
- 1 clove of garlic, minced
- 1 cup of feta cheese, crumbled and extra for sprinkling
- 1 zucchini, chopped
- 1 cup of cherry tomatoes, cut into quarters
- ½ cup of Kalamata olives, chopped
- 2 tablespoons of dill, chopped
- Lemon wedges, sliced and for serving

ooooooooooooooooooooooooooooooooooooooooo

Procedure:

A. Preheat the oven to 350°F.

B. Slice the tops off of each bell pepper. Remove the insides and place them into a large baking dish.

C. In a large skillet set over medium heat, add a tablespoon of olive oil. Once hot, add in the chicken. Season with a dash of salt, black pepper, and dried oregano. Cook for 8 to 10 minutes on each side or until golden brown. Remove and set aside to rest for 5 minutes.

D. In a medium saucepan set over medium to high heat, add one cup of the chicken broth. Bring the broth to a boil. Remove from heat and add in the couscous. Set aside for 5 to 10 minutes or until the couscous is soft.

E. In a large bowl, add the cooked couscous, chopped red onion, minced garlic, ½ cup of the crumbled feta cheese, and the chopped zucchini. Stir well to mix. Season with a dash of salt and black pepper.

F. Spoon the couscous mixture into the insides of the bell peppers. Top off with the remaining half cup of crumbled feta cheese.

G. Pour the remaining chicken broth into the baking dish and cover.

H. Place into the oven to bake for 45 minutes or until the bell peppers are soft.

I. Remove and drizzle fresh lemon juice over the top of each pepper. Serve immediately.

4. Greek Moussaka

Yield: 6 servings

Cooking Time: 1 hour and 10 minutes

Ingredients for the eggplant:

- 2 eggplants, cut into ¼ inch slices
- 2 tablespoons of extra virgin olive oil

Ingredients for the filling:

- 1 tablespoon of extra virgin olive oil
- 1 onion, chopped
- 2 cloves of garlic, minced
- 4 pound of lean ground beef
- 1, 14 ounces can of tomatoes, crushed
- 3 tablespoons of tomato paste
- 1 cup of beef broth
- 1 ½ teaspoon of white sugar
- 2 teaspoons of dried oregano
- ¾ teaspoons of salt

Ingredients for the sauce:

- 4 tablespoons of butter
- 5 tablespoons of all-purpose flour
- 3 cups of whole milk
- ¼ teaspoons of grated nutmeg
- ½ cup grated Parmesan cheese
- 1 egg, beaten
- 1 egg yolk
- A dash of salt and black pepper

Ingredients for topping:

- 1/3 cup of panko breadcrumbs

ooooooooooooooooooooooooooooooooooooooooo

Procedure:

A. Season the eggplant with a dash of salt and place into a colander. Set aside to sweat for 30 minutes. Pat dry with a few paper towels.

B. Preheat the oven to 400°F. Place the eggplant onto two large baking sheets. Brush the eggplants with olive oil. Place into the oven to bake for 10 minutes or until soft. Remove and set aside to cool completely.

C. In a large skillet set over medium to high heat, add 1 tablespoon of olive oil. Once hot, add the minced garlic and chopped onion. Cook for 3 to 5 minutes or until soft.

D. Add in the ground beef and break it apart with a wooden spoon. Add in the remaining ingredients for the filling. Stir well to mix. Cook for 15 minutes or until the beef is cooked through. Remove from heat and set aside.

E. In a separate large saucepan set over medium heat, add the butter. Once melted, add the all-purpose flour. Whisk until smooth in consistency. Add in one cup of whole milk and whisk to mix. Cook for 3 to 5 minutes or until thick in consistency. Remove from heat.

F. Add in the grated Parmesan cheese. Whisk until melted and set aside for 5 minutes. Add in the eggs and whisk to mix.

G. Preheat the oven to 350°F.

H. Place the eggplant into a large baking dish. Fill to the top with the filling. Place the remaining eggplant over the top. Pour the béchamel sauce over the top.

I. Sprinkle the breadcrumbs over the eggplant.

J. Place into the oven to bake for 30 to 40 minutes or until golden brown. Remove and set aside to stand for 10 minutes. Serve.

5. Garlic Greek Chicken

Yield: 4 servings

Cooking Time: 50 minutes

Ingredient List:

- 3 tablespoons of extra virgin olive oil, evenly divided
- 1 lemon, juice only
- 3 cloves of garlic, minced
- 1 teaspoon of dried oregano
- 1 pound of chicken thighs, bone-in
- A dash of salt and black pepper
- ½ pound of asparagus, ends torn off
- 1 zucchini, sliced into rounds
- 1 lemon, thinly sliced

OOOOOOOOOOOOOOOOOOOOOOOOOOOOOOOOOOOOOOOOOO

Procedure:

A. In a large bowl, add two tablespoons of olive oil, fresh lemon juice, minced garlic, and dried oregano. Whisk until evenly mixed. Add in the chicken thighs. Toss to mix. Cover and set the chicken aside to marinate for 15 minutes.

B. Preheat the oven to 425°F.

C. In a cast iron skillet set over medium to high heat, add one tablespoon of olive oil.

D. Season the chicken thighs with a dash of salt and black pepper. Add into the skillet with the skin side facing down. Pour the marinade over the top. Cook for 10 minutes on each side or until seared.

E. Add in the asparagus, zucchini rounds, and sliced lemon.

F. Transfer into the oven to bake for 15 minutes or until the chicken is cooked through.

G. Remove and serve immediately.

6. Classic Hummus

Yield: 16 servings

Cooking Time: 10 minutes

Ingredient List:

- 2 cups of garbanzo beans, drained
- 1/3 cup of tahini
- ¼ cup of lemon juice
- 1 teaspoon of salt
- 2 cloves of garlic, cut into halves
- 1 tablespoon of extra virgin olive oil
- A dash of smoked paprika
- 1 teaspoon of parsley, minced

OOOOOOOOOOOOOOOOOOOOOOOOOOOOOOOOOOOOOOOO

Procedure:

A. In a food processor, add the drained garbanzo beans, tahini, fresh lemon juice, dash of salt, and garlic halves. Blend on the highest setting until smooth in consistency. Transfer this mixture to a medium bowl.

B. Drizzle the olive oil over the top.

C. Serve with a sprinkling of minced garlic and a dash of smoked paprika.

7. Greek Honey Cake

Yield: 12 servings

Cooking Time: 1 hour and 10 minutes

Ingredient List:

- 1 cup of all-purpose flour
- 1 ½ teaspoon of baking powder
- ¼ teaspoons of salt
- ½ teaspoons of ground cinnamon
- 1 teaspoon of orange zest
- ¾ cup of butter, soft
- ¾ cup of white sugar
- 3 eggs, beaten
- ¼ cup of whole milk
- 1 cup of walnuts, chopped
- 1 cup of white sugar
- 1 cup of honey
- ¾ cup of water
- 1 teaspoon of lemon juice

OOOOOOOOOOOOOOOOOOOOOOOOOOOOOOOOOOOOOOOOOOOO

Procedure:

Preheat the oven to 350°F. Grease a large cake pan and dust it with flour.

In a large bowl, add the all-purpose flour, salt, fresh orange zest, ground cinnamon, and baking powder. Stir well to mix and set this mixture aside.

In a separate large bowl, add the soft butter and ¾ cup of white sugar. Beat with an electric mixer until fluffy in consistency. Add in the beaten eggs, whole milk, and flour mixture. Continue to beat until just mixed.

Pour the batter into the cake pan. Place into the oven to bake for 40 minutes or until baked through. Remove and cool for 15 minutes.

In a small saucepan set over medium heat, add the honey, 1 cup of white sugar, and water. Stir well to mix and cook for 5 minutes. Bring the mixture to a boil. Continue to cook for 2 minutes. Remove from heat.

Pour the honey syrup over the top of the cake. Serve immediately.

8. Greek Shrimp and Tomatoes

Yield: 4 servings

Cooking Time: 50 minutes

Ingredient List:

- 4 tablespoons of extra virgin olive oil
- ¾ cup of shallots, chopped
- 4 cloves of garlic, chopped
- 1, 28 ounces can of tomatoes, chopped
- 1 ½ teaspoons of salt
- ¼ teaspoons of black pepper
- 1 teaspoon of ground cumin
- ½ teaspoons of crushed red pepper flakes
- 1 tablespoon of honey
- 1 ½ pound of shrimp, peeled and deveined
- 6 ounces of feta cheese, crumbled
- ¾ teaspoons of dried oregano
- 2 tablespoons of mint, chopped

OOOOOOOOOOOOOOOOOOOOOOOOOOOOOOOOOOOOOOOOOOOO

Procedure:

A. Preheat the oven to 400°F.

B. In a large skillet set over low to medium heat, add the olive oil. Once hot, add in the shallots and chopped garlic. Cook for 5 to 8 minutes or until soft.

C. In the can of tomatoes, ground cumin, crushed red pepper flakes, and honey. Season with a dash of salt and black pepper. Stir well to mix and bring the mixture to a boil. Reduce the heat to low. Cook for 15 to 20 minutes or until thick in consistency.

D. Place the shrimp over the tomato sauce mixture. Add the crumbled feta cheese over the top and season with the dried oregano.

E. Place into the oven to bake for 10 to 15 minutes or until the shrimp is bright pink.

F. Increase the temperature of the oven to broil. Broil for 1 to 2 minutes or until the cheese is golden brown.

G. Remove and cool for 5 minutes before serving.

9. Greek Lentil Soup

Yield: 4 servings

Cooking Time: 1 hour and 20 minutes

Ingredient List:

- 8 ounces of brown lentils
- ¼ cup of extra virgin olive oil
- 1 tablespoon of garlic, minced
- 1 onion, minced
- 1 carrot, chopped
- 1 quart of water
- A dash of dried oregano
- A pinch of dried rosemary
- 2 bay leaves
- 1 tablespoon of tomato paste
- A dash of salt and black pepper
- 1 teaspoon of extra virgin olive oil
- 1 teaspoon of red wine vinegar, optional

OOOOOOOOOOOOOOOOOOOOOOOOOOOOOOOOOOOOOOOOO

Procedure:

A. In a large saucepan set over medium heat, add in the lentils and cover with water. Once the water begins to boil, reduce the heat to low. Cook for 10 minutes or until soft.

B. In a large saucepan placed over medium heat, add the olive oil. Once hot, add in the minced garlic, minced onion, and chopped carrot. Stir well to mix. Cook for 5 minutes or until soft.

C. Add in the brown lentils, 1 quart of water, dried oregano, dried rosemary, and bay leaves. Make sure to stir everything well to mix and bring the mixture to a boil over the heat. Reduce the heat to low. Cover and cook for 10 minutes.

D. Add in the tomato paste. Season with a dash of salt and black pepper.

E. Cover and continue to simmer for 30 to 40 minutes or until the brown lentils are soft.

F. Drizzle the remaining teaspoon of olive oil and red vinegar over the top.

G. Remove from heat and serve immediately.

10. Greek Quesadillas

Yield: 4 servings

Cooking Time: 25 minutes

Ingredients for the sauce:

- 1 cup of Greek yogurt
- ½ of a cucumber, chopped
- 1 tablespoon of dill, chopped
- ½ of a lemon, juice and extra if needed
- A dash of salt and black pepper
- A dash of crushed red pepper flakes
- Ingredients for the quesadillas:
- 1 tablespoon of extra virgin olive oil
- 4 pitas, cut into halves
- 3 cups of mozzarella cheese, shredded
- 2 cups of chicken, shredded
- 1 cup of feta cheese, crumbled
- ½ cup of red bell peppers, roasted and drained
- ½ cup of Kalamata olives, chopped
- 1 tablespoon of dill, chopped

OOOOOOOOOOOOOOOOOOOOOOOOOOOOOOOOOOOOOOOOO

Procedure:

A. In a medium bowl, add all of the ingredients for the sauce. Whisk until evenly mixed. Set the sauce aside.

B. In a large skillet set over medium heat, add one tablespoon of olive oil. One hot, add in one pita half. On each pita half, sprinkle the mozzarella cheese and shredded chicken over the top. Sprinkle the crumbled feta cheese, red bell pepper slice, sliced olives, and chopped dill over the top of this mixture.

C. Cook for 2 minutes. Cover with another pita half. Turn over the pita and continue to cook for another 2 minutes or until golden.

D. Repeat with the remaining pitas and ingredients.

E. Serve with a drizzling of the sauce over the top.

11. Greek Chicken Pasta

Yield: 6 servings

Cooking Time: 30 minutes

Ingredient List:

- 1 pound of penne pasta
- A dash of salt and black pepper
- A splash of extra virgin olive oil
- ¾ pound of chicken breasts, boneless and skinless
- 1 teaspoon of dried oregano
- 2 cloves of garlic, minced
- ¾ cup of half and half
- 8 ounces of cream cheese
- ½ cup of feta cheese, crumbled
- 1 tablespoon of lemon juice
- 1 teaspoon of lemon zest
- 1 ½ cup of cherry tomatoes, cut into halves
- ½ cup of Kalamata olives, pitted and cut into halves
- 1 cucumber, chopped
- ¼ cup of dill, chopped
- Parsley, chopped and for serving

OOOOOOOOOOOOOOOOOOOOOOOOOOOOOOOOOOOOOOOOOO

Procedure:

A. Prepare the pasta according to the directions on the package. Once cooked, drain the pasta and set aside.

B. In a large skillet set over medium heat, add one tablespoon of olive oil.

C. Season the chicken with a dash of salt, dried oregano, and black pepper. Place into the skillet and cook for 8 to 10 minutes on each side or until cooked through. Remove and set aside to rest for 5 to 10 minutes.

D. Add another tablespoon of olive oil. Once hot, add the minced garlic. Cook for 1 minute or until fragrant. Add in the half-and-half, soft cream cheese, and crumbled feta cheese. Stir well to mix. Cook for 1 minute or until melted.

E. Add in the lemon juice and lemon zest. Season with a dash of salt and black pepper.

F. Add in the pasta, cherry tomato halves, Kalamata olive halves, chopped cucumber, and chopped dill. Toss well until evenly mixed.

G. Remove from heat. Serve with a garnish of chopped parsley.

12. Greek Lemon Chicken Soup

Yield: 16 servings

Cooking Time: 1 hour and 5 minutes

Ingredient List:

- 8 cups of chicken broth
- ½ cup of lemon juice
- ½ cup of carrots, shredded
- ½ cup of onion, chopped
- ½ cup of celery, chopped
- 6 tablespoons of chicken soup base
- ¼ teaspoons of white pepper
- ¼ cup of margarine, soft
- ¼ cup of all-purpose flour
- 1 cup of white rice, cooked
- 1 cup of chicken, cooked and chopped
- 16 lemon slices
- 8 egg yolks

OOOOOOOOOOOOOOOOOOOOOOOOOOOOOOOOOOOOOOOOO

Procedure:

A. In a large pot set over high heat, add the chicken broth, fresh lemon juice, shredded carrot, chopped onion, chopped celery, soup base, and a dash of white pepper. Stir well to mix and bring to a boil. Reduce the heat to low and simmer for 20 minutes.

B. In a large bowl, add the soft margarine and all-purpose flour. Stir well until just mixed.

C. Transfer the flour mixture to the soup mixture. Stir well to incorporate and continue to cook for another 10 minutes.

D. In a medium bowl, add the egg white. Beat for 3 minutes or until pale. Add into the soup mixture slowly. Stir well to mix.

E. Add in the cooked white rice and chopped chicken. Continue to cook for an additional minute or until hot.

F. Remove from heat. Serve with a garnish of lemon slices.

13. Greek New Year's Cake

Yield: 12 servings

Cooking Time: 1 hour and 30 minutes

Ingredient List:

- Butter - 1 cup
- White sugar - 2 cups
- Flour - 3 cups
- 6 eggs, beaten
- 2 teaspoons of baker's style baking powder
- 1 cup of warm milk
- ½ teaspoons of baker's style baking soda
- 1 tablespoon of lemon juice
- ¼ cup of almonds, cut into slivers
- 2 tablespoons of white sugar

OOOOOOOOOOOOOOOOOOOOOOOOOOOOOOOOOOOOOOOOOOO

Procedure:

A. Preheat the oven to 350°F. Grease a large cake pan.

B. In a medium bowl, add the butter and white sugar. Beat with an electric mixer until creamy in consistency. Add in the all-purpose flour and stir well until mixed. Add in the beaten eggs and beat again.

C. Add in the baking powder, whole milk, fresh lemon juice, and baking soda. Stir well to mix.

D. Pour the cake batter into the cake pan.

E. Place into the oven to bake for 20 minutes. Remove and sprinkle the almond slicers and the remaining two tablespoons of sugar over the taste. Place back into the oven to bake for 20 to 30 minutes or until baked through.

F. Remove and place the cake onto a wire rack to cool for 10 minutes before serving.

14. Greek Feta and Spinach Pinwheels

Yield: 12 to 20 servings

Cooking Time: 45 minutes

Ingredient List:

- 1 egg yolk + 1 tablespoon of water, whisked together
- ½ cup of feta cheese, crumbled
- ¼ cup of mozzarella cheese, grated
- 1 green onion, chopped
- ½ teaspoons of garlic salt
- A dash of grated nutmeg
- 1, 10 ounce pack of spinach, chopped
- 1 sheet of puff pastry, frozen and thawed

OOOOOOOOOOOOOOOOOOOOOOOOOOOOOOOOOOOOOOOOOO

Procedure:

A. In a medium bowl, add in the crumbled feta cheese, grated mozzarella cheese, chopped onion, garlic salt and grated nutmeg. Stir well to mix and set this mixture aside.

B. Place the puff pastry sheet onto a flat surface dusted with flour. Brush with the egg wash and pour the cheese mixture over the top.

C. Top off with the chopped spinach.

D. Roll the pastry around the filling jelly roll Slice the roll into ¾ inch slices and place the pinwheels onto two baking sheets lined with parchment paper. Set into the fridge to chill.

E. Preheat the oven to 400°F.

F. Place the pinwheels into the oven to bake for 15 minutes or until golden brown.

G. Remove and cool for 5 minutes before serving.

15. Greek Butter Cookies

Yield: 48 servings

Cooking Time: 20 minutes

Ingredient List:

- 1 cup of butter, soft
- ¾ cup of white sugar
- 1 egg, beaten
- Pure vanilla - ½ teaspoon
- ½ teaspoon of almond extract
- 2 ¼ cups of all-purpose flour
- ½ cup of powdered sugar

OOOOOOOOOOOOOOOOOOOOOOOOOOOOOOOOOOOOOOOOOO

Procedure:

A. Preheat the oven to 400°F. Grease two large cookie sheets with cooking spray.

B. In a medium bowl, add the butter, white sugar, and beaten egg. Beat with an electric mixer until smooth in consistency. Add in the pure vanilla and almond extract. Beat again to mix.

C. Add in the all-purpose flour and stir well until a dough begins to form.

D. Take a teaspoon of the dough and roll it into balls. Shape the balls into 8 shapes. Repeat with the remaining balls and place them onto the greased cookie sheets.

E. Place into the oven to bake for 10 minutes or until light brown.

F. Remove and cool for 10 minutes. Dust with the powdered sugar and serve immediately.

16. Greek Spinach Pie

Yield: 5 servings

Cooking Time: 1 hour and 30 minutes

Ingredient List:

- 3 tablespoons of extra virgin olive oil
- 1 onion, chopped
- 1 bunch of green onions, chopped
- 2 cloves of garlic, minced
- 2 pounds of spinach, chopped
- ½ cup of parsley, chopped
- 2 eggs, beaten
- ½ cup of ricotta cheese
- 1 cup of feta cheese, crumbled
- 8 sheets of phyllo dough
- ¼ cup of extra virgin olive oil

OOOOOOOOOOOOOOOOOOOOOOOOOOOOOOOOOOOOOOOOO

Procedure:

A. Preheat the oven to 350°F. Grease a large baking dish with cooking spray.

B. In a large skillet set over medium heat, add three tablespoons of olive oil. Once hot, add in the chopped onion, chopped green onions, and minced garlic. Cook for 5 minutes or until soft.

C. Add in the chopped spinach and chopped parsley. Stir well to mix and continue to cook for 2 minutes. Remove the mixture from the heat and set it aside.

D. In a medium bowl, add the beaten eggs, ricotta cheese, and crumbled feta cheese. Stir well to mix before adding in the spinach mixture. Continue to stir until mixed.

E. Place a phyllo sheet into the greased baking dish. Brush with olive oil. Add another phyllo sheet over the top. Brush again with olive oil. Repeat with two more phyllo sheets. Spread the spinach mixture over the phyllo sheets. Place 4 more sheets of phyllo over the filling, making sure to spread olive oil over each sheet.

F. Place into the oven to bake for 30 to 40 minutes or until golden brown.

G. Remove and cut into squares. Serve.

17. Greek Lemon Cake

Yield: 12 servings

Cooking Time: 1 hour and 30 minutes

Ingredient List:

- 3 cups of cake flour
- 1 teaspoon of baking soda
- ¼ teaspoons of salt
- 6 eggs, whites and yolks separated
- 2 cups of white sugar, evenly divided
- 1 cup of butter, soft
- 2 teaspoons of lemon zest, grated
- 2 tablespoons of lemon juice
- 1 cup of whole plain yogurt

OOOOOOOOOOOOOOOOOOOOOOOOOOOOOOOOOOOOOOOOOO

Procedure:

A. Preheat the oven to 350°F. Grease a large tube pan with cooking spray.

B. In a large bowl, add the cake flour, salt, and baking soda. Stir well to mix and set the mixture aside.

C. In a large bowl, add the egg whites. Beat with an electric mixer on the highest setting until peaks begin to form on the surface. Add in ½ cup of white sugar. Continue to beat until the peaks are stiff. Set this mixture aside.

D. In a separate large bowl, add the butter and the remaining 1 ½ cups of white sugar. Beat with an electric mixer until fluffy in consistency. Add in the egg yolks, fresh lemon juice, and zest. Beat until evenly mixed.

E. Add in the flour mixture and continue to beat until just mixed. Add in the beaten egg whites. Fold gently until incorporated.

F. Pour the batter into the greased tube pan. Place into the oven to bake for 1 hour or until baked through. Remove and cool for 10 minutes before inverting onto a wire rack to cool completely.

18. Baked Greek Salmon

Yield: 4 servings

Cooking Time: 25 minutes

Ingredient List:

- 4 salmon filets, skin removed
- 1 teaspoon of extra virgin olive oil
- ¼ teaspoons of salt
- ½ teaspoons of black pepper
- 1 lemon, thinly sliced
- 2 cloves of garlic thinly sliced
- 8 sprigs of thyme
- 4 tomatoes, chopped

OOOOOOOOOOOOOOOOOOOOOOOOOOOOOOOOOOOOOOOOOOO

Procedure:

A. Preheat the oven to 475°F.
B. Season the salmon filets on both sides with a dash of salt and black pepper. Drizzle the olive oil over the top.
C. Grease a medium baking dish with olive oil. Add in the salmon filets.
D. Top off with lemon slices, garlic slices, and thyme. Scatter the chopped tomatoes over the top.
E. Place into the oven to bake for 15 to 20 minutes or until cooked through.
F. Remove and cool for 5 minutes before serving.

19. Greek Pasta

Yield: 4 servings

Cooking Time: 2 hours and 15 minutes

Ingredient List:

- 1 yellow onion, chopped
- 1 tablespoon of extra virgin olive oil
- 5 cloves of garlic, minced
- 1, 16 ounces can of Italian tomatoes, chopped
- 1, 5.6 ounces can of tomato sauce
- 1 tablespoon of capers, chopped
- 15 Kalamata olives, pitted and thinly sliced
- 2 tablespoons of balsamic vinegar
- A dash of salt and black pepper
- A dash of crushed red pepper flakes, optional
- Feta cheese, crumbled

OOOOOOOOOOOOOOOOOOOOOOOOOOOOOOOOOOOOOOOOO

Procedure:

A. In a large skillet set over medium to high heat, add the extra virgin olive oil. Once hot, add in the onion. Cook for 5 minutes or until soft.
B. Add in the minced garlic and then cook for an additional minute.
C. Add in the chopped tomatoes, can of tomato sauce, chopped capers, sliced olives, balsamic vinegar, a dash of salt, a dash of black pepper, and crushed red pepper flakes. Stir well to mix.
D. Reduce the heat to low and cook for 30 minutes.
E. Remove from heat and serve over a bed of spaghetti.

20. Greek Wedding Soup

Yield: 4 servings

Cooking Time: 50 minutes

Ingredient List:

- ½ pound of lean ground beef
- ¼ cup of feta cheese, crumbled
- 2 tablespoons of plain breadcrumbs
- 3 eggs, large
- 2 cloves of garlic, chopped
- 2 tablespoons of mint leaves, chopped
- ½ teaspoons of salt
- ¼ teaspoons of black pepper
- 1, 32-ounce carton of chicken broth
- 2 carrots, peeled and sliced
- 1/3 cup of orzo pasta
- 3 cups baby spinach, chopped
- 1 tablespoon of lemon juice
- Mizithra cheese, shredded

OOOOOOOOOOOOOOOOOOOOOOOOOOOOOOOOOOOOOOOOOOOOO

Procedure:

A. In a large bowl, add the ground beef, crumbled feta cheese, plain breadcrumbs, 1 egg, chopped garlic, and chopped mint leaves. Season with a dash of salt and black pepper. Stir well to mix and shape this mixture into 1-inch

B. In a medium saucepan set over high heat, add the chicken broth. Bring the broth to a boil. Reduce the heat to medium. Add in the meatballs, sliced carrots, and orzo pasta. Stir well to mix. Continue to cook for 10 to 12 minutes or until your meatballs are soft.

C. Add in the spinach and continue to cook for 1 to 2 minutes.

D. In a medium bowl, add the remaining 2 eggs and fresh lemon juice. Whisk until evenly mixed and foamy. Add in 1 cup of the hot stock and whisk until mixed. Pour this mixture into the saucepan with the meatballs. Cook for 2 minutes or until thick in consistency.

E. Remove and serve with a topping of shredded Mizithra cheese.

21. One Pan Greek Chicken and Lemon Rice

Yield: 5 servings

Cooking Time: 1 hour

Ingredients for the chicken:

- 5 chicken thighs, skin on and bone in
- 1 to 2 lemons, zest and juice only
- 1 tablespoon of dried oregano
- 4 cloves of garlic, minced
- ½ teaspoons of salt

Ingredients for the rice:

- 1 ½ tablespoons of extra virgin olive oil, evenly separated
- 1 onion, chopped
- 1 cup of long grain white rice
- 1 ½ cups of chicken broth
- ¾ cup of water
- 1 tablespoon of dried oregano
- ¾ teaspoons of salt
- A dash of black pepper

Ingredients for garnish:

- Parsley, chopped and optional
- Lemon zest

OOOOOOOOOOOOOOOOOOOOOOOOOOOOOOOOOOOOOOOOO

Procedure:

A. In a large Ziploc bag, add all of the ingredients for the chicken. Stir well to mix and set aside and let it marinate for 20 minutes.

B. Preheat the oven to 350°F.

C. Remove the chicken from the marinade and set aside.

D. In a large skillet set over medium to high heat, add half a tablespoon of olive oil. Once hot, add in the chicken. Cook for 8 to 10 minutes on each side or until it turns golden brown. Remove the chicken and set aside.

E. Pour the excess grease from the skillet. Clean out with a few paper towels. Add another tablespoon of olive oil to the skillet. Once hot, add in the chopped onion. Cook for 5 minutes or until soft. Add in the rice, chicken broth, water, and dried oregano. Season with a dash of salt and black pepper. Stir well to mix.

F. Place the chicken on top of the rice mixture. Cover and transfer into the oven to bake for 35 minutes. Remove the cover and continue to bake for 10 minutes.

G. Remove from the oven and rest for 10 minutes. Serve with a garnish of oregano, chopped parsley, and lemon zest.

22. Greek Chicken Gyros

Yield: 6 servings

Cooking Time: 3 hours

Ingredient List:

- 2 pounds of chicken breasts, skinless and boneless
- ¼ cup of extra virgin olive oil, extra for brushing
- ¼ cup of lemon juice
- 3 tablespoons of plain Greek yogurt
- 1 tablespoon of red wine vinegar
- 1/3 cup of red onion, chopped
- 2 cloves of garlic, minced
- 1 ½ teaspoon of dried oregano
- 1 teaspoon of dried thyme
- ½ teaspoons of coriander
- Dash of salt and black pepper

Ingredients for serving:

- 6 to 8 pita flatbreads, store-bought
- Tzatziki sauce
- Feta cheese, crumbled
- Cilantro, chopped

OOOOOOOOOOOOOOOOOOOOOOOOOOOOOOOOOOOOOOOO

Procedure:

A. In a large bowl, add in the extra virgin olive oil, lemon juice, plain yogurt, vinegar, red onion, minced garlic, dried oregano, dried thyme, coriander and a dash of black pepper and salt. Stir well to mix.

B. In a large Ziploc bag, add in the chicken. Pour the marinade over the top.

C. Seal the bag and place into the fridge to marinate for 2 to 4 hours.

D. Grease the grates of an outdoor grill to medium with oil. Preheat the grill to medium or high heat. Once hot, place the chicken onto the grill. Grill for 10 minutes on each side or until cooked through.

E. Remove and set aside while covered to rest for 10 minutes. Slice the chicken into thin strips.

F. Place the chicken slices onto the flatbreads. Top off with the crumbled feta cheese and chopped cilantro. Drizzle the tzatziki sauce over the top. Wrap tightly and serve immediately.

Yield: 4 servings

Cooking Time: 15 minutes

Ingredient List:

- 4 cloves of garlic, unpeeled
- 1 ¼ pound of lean ground lamb
- ½ cup of feta cheese, crumbled
- ¾ teaspoons of dried oregano
- ½ teaspoons of salt
- ½ teaspoons of black pepper
- ½ of a cucumber, peeled and grated
- ¾ cup of sour cream
- 1 tablespoon of mint, minced
- 1 teaspoon of rice wine vinegar
- 1 clove of garlic, minced
- 4 red onion slices
- 4 tomato slices
- 4, 4-inch pita bread

ooooooooooooooooooooooooooooooooooooooooooo

Procedure:

A. In a small skillet set over medium to high heat, add the cloves of garlic. Cook for 5 minutes or until browned. Mince the garlic and set aside.

B. In a medium bowl, add the lamb. Sprinkle the roasted minced garlic, crumbled feta cheese, dried oregano, a dash of salt, and a dash of black pepper. Stir well to mix.

C. Divide the meat mixture into 4 pieces. Form the pieces into balls. Flatten slightly into patties that are 4 inches in width.

D. In a small bowl, add the grated cucumber, sour cream, minced mint, rice vinegar, one clove of minced garlic, a dash of salt, and a dash of black pepper. Stir well to mix and set into the fridge to chill until ready to serve.

E. Preheat an outdoor grill to medium or high heat. Add in the burger patties. Cover and cook for 5-6 minutes on each side or until it is cooked through.

F. Add the pitas to the grill. Cook for 1 minute on each side or until grilled.

G. Spread 1 to 2 tablespoons of the sauce over the pita bread. Top off with a slice of onion, a tomato slice, and one of the cooked burgers. Spread a tablespoon of the remaining sauce over the top. Top off with the remaining pita halves and serve immediately.

24. Baked Greek White Fish

Yield: 1 serving

Cooking Time: 45 minutes

Ingredient List:

- 1, 8 to 9 ounce Swai filet
- 1 tablespoon of lemon juice
- 1 ½ tablespoon of butter, melted
- ½ teaspoons of Greek seasoning
- 1 tablespoon of roasted red bell pepper, chopped
- 1 tablespoon of French fried onions, crushed
- 1 tablespoon of parsley, chopped

OOOOOOOOOOOOOOOOOOOOOOOOOOOOOOOOOOOOOOOOOO

Procedure:

A. Preheat the oven to 400°F. Line a large baking sheet with a sheet of aluminum foil. Place the Swai filet onto the baking sheet.
B. Drizzle the fresh lemon juice and melted butter over the filet. Season with Greek seasoning. Season with a dash of salt and black pepper.
C. Add the roasted red bell pepper, crushed onions, and parsley over the top.
D. Place into the oven to bake for 30 minutes.
E. Remove and serve immediately.

25. 30 Minute Greek Chicken with Greek Sauce

Yield: 4 servings

Cooking Time: 30 minutes

Ingredient List:

- 2 tablespoons of extra virgin olive oil
- 4 chicken breasts, boneless, skinless and cut into halves
- 1 cup of low sodium chicken stock
- 2 eggs, beaten
- 1 lemon, juice and zest only
- A dash of salt and black pepper
- Parsley, chopped and for garnish

ooooooooooooooooooooooooooooooooooooooooo

Procedure:

In a large skillet set over medium to high heat, add in the oil. Once the oil is hot, add in the chicken. Cook for 8 to 10 minutes or until golden brown on all sides. Remove and set aside on a plate. Keep warm.

Add the low-sodium chicken stock into the skillet. Deglaze the bottom of the pan.

In a medium bowl, add the eggs. Whisk until lightly beaten. Add in the fresh lemon juice and lemon zest. Whisk again to mix.

Add half a cup of the hot broth to the beaten eggs. Stir well until mixed. Pour the egg mixture into the skillet and stir well to mix. Cook for 3 minutes or until thick in consistency. Season with a dash of salt and black pepper.

Strain the hot broth through a fine mesh strainer into a medium bowl.

Serve the chicken with the sauce poured over the top. Garnish with chopped parsley.

Author's Note

Not many people do this, but I grew up under difficult circumstances where nothing was handed to me, and the only way forward was with your best effort. At some point, people started recognizing me for my talent in the kitchen despite my young age, and I've only worked harder from there!

Because I am constantly trying to improve my work, I would really appreciate your help. Sure, I always ask my friends and family for their feedback on my newest projects but, whether they want to accept it or not, there's always some sort of bias because they don't want to hurt my feelings by criticizing my work. Thus, I need a neutral pair of eyes — that's where you come in!

If you're up for it, I would appreciate you telling me what you think of my cookbooks. Are the recipes easy to follow? Did you get stuck somewhere? Are the measurements laid out? Any suggestions you may have are welcome. After all, cookbooks are only helpful when you actually understand them! Incorporating your ideas and suggestions into my new projects will be my show of eternal gratitude because you can only be the best at something by constantly improving and being open to change.

Thanks!

Alicia T. White

About the Author

Alicia had a tough childhood and had to take care of her siblings early. Although they often helped her with making the beds and washing, Alicia was responsible for cooking since she was the oldest of six. Being in the kitchen was still very difficult at her age, but she learned her way around the stove and oven throughout the years.

Whereas her first dishes were practically inedible, burnt rice and mushy pasta… Eventually, she turned to the oven for help as many of the dishes she wanted to make were too complicated. Nonetheless, her baked casseroles were amazing! Most importantly, they were simple and required way less clean-up.

At first, they were simple pasta bakes, but once Alicia got the hang of things, she was baking all sorts of meals. When it came to spreading the word of her delicious cooking, having 5 siblings was extremely advantageous. Soon, neighbors were placing orders for some of her casseroles! Eventually, Alicia was doing so well with the business that she hired extra help. Now it's one of the most affordable yet popular weeknight casserole services in the mid-West!

Today, she still lives with her siblings and is working hard to teach them about the family business that led them out of poverty. She likes to publish cookbooks on casseroles and one-pot meals in her free time— basically anything quick and easy. Her motto is, "If a seven-year-old can't make it, it isn't simple enough!"